No. 9973

Rock with Jazz

Book Two

Piano Solos

by
Melvin Stecher
Norman Horowitz
and
Claire Gordon

ISBN 0-7935-4946-9

G. SCHIRMER, *Inc.*

DISTRIBUTED BY

HAL•LEONARD®
CORPORATION
7777 W. BLUEMOUND RD. P.O. BOX 13819 MILWAUKEE, WI 53213

T0050916

THE HIPPY POTAMUS

Moderately fast, with a steady beat

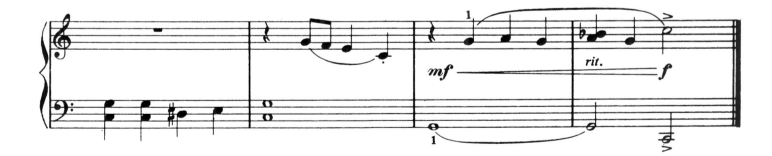

ELECTRIC FAN-FARE

THE WEASEL GOES POP

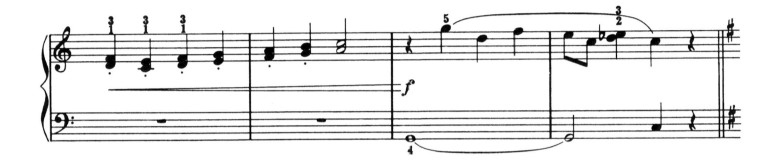

SOLID ROCK

With a steady rock beat

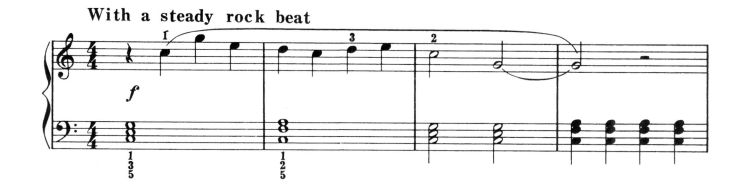

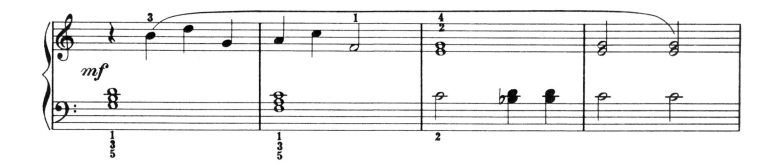

KIN-FOLK

Lively, with a bounce

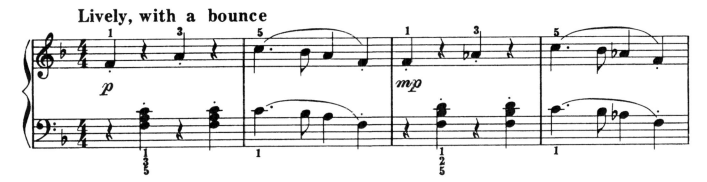

LITTLE LP

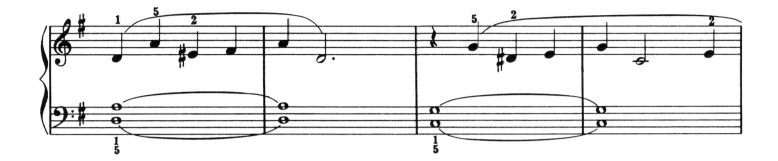

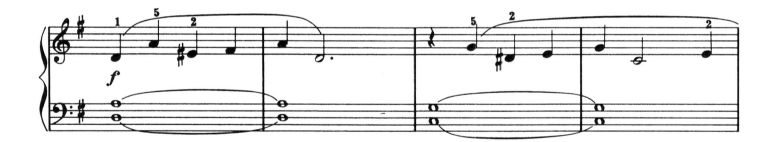

OUT OF THE BLUES

Moderate blues tempo

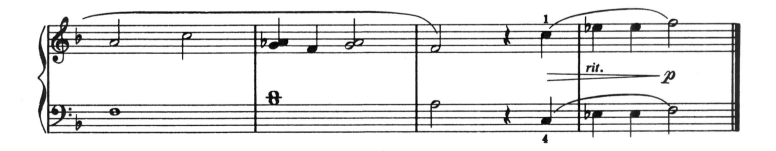

LEMON 'N' LIME POP

Lively

ROCK 'EM, COWBOY

With a steady rock beat

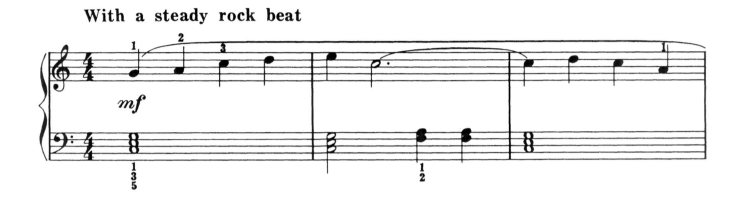

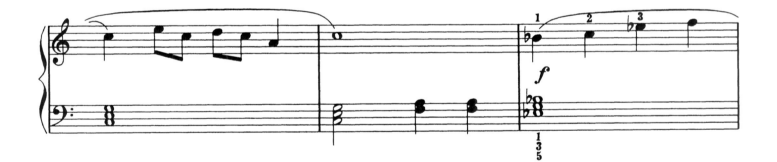

SUPERSONIC TONIC

Moderately fast

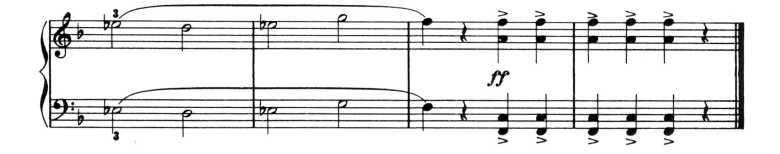